W

Flash AND gleam

LIGHT IN OUR WORLD

SUE FLIESS
Illustrated by **KHOA LE**

Millbrook Press / Minneapolis

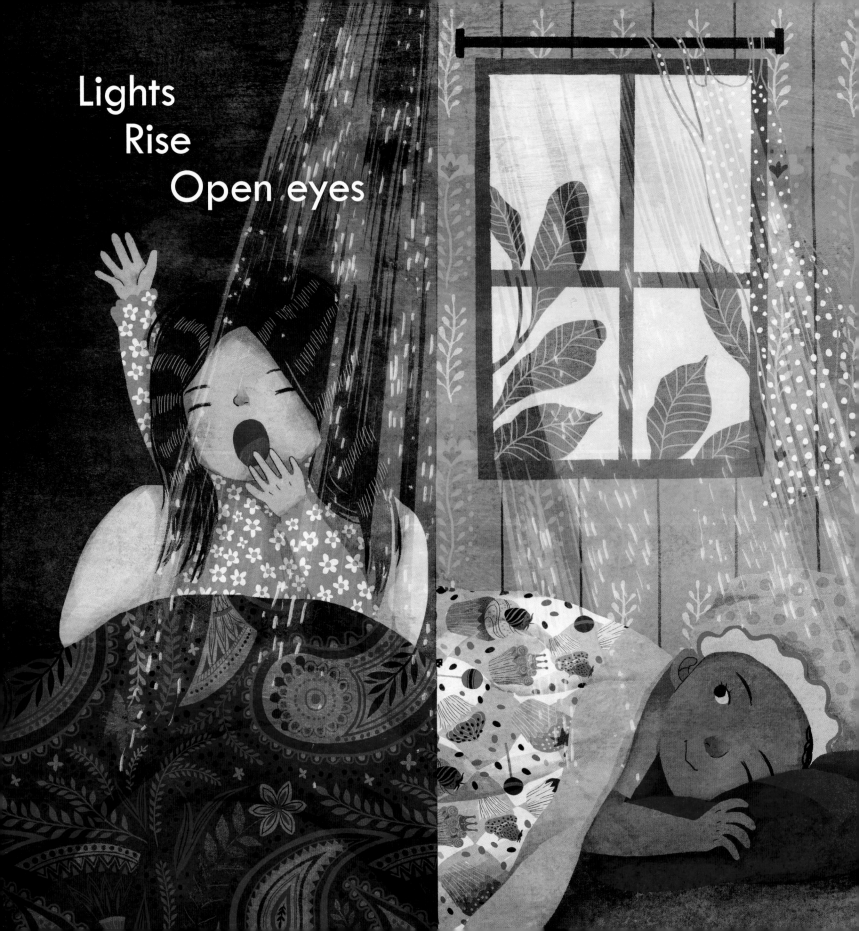

Lights
Rise
Open eyes

שָׁלוֹם

Reach
Low
Nurture, grow

Bolt
Flash
Thunder crash

Color
Bend
Find the end

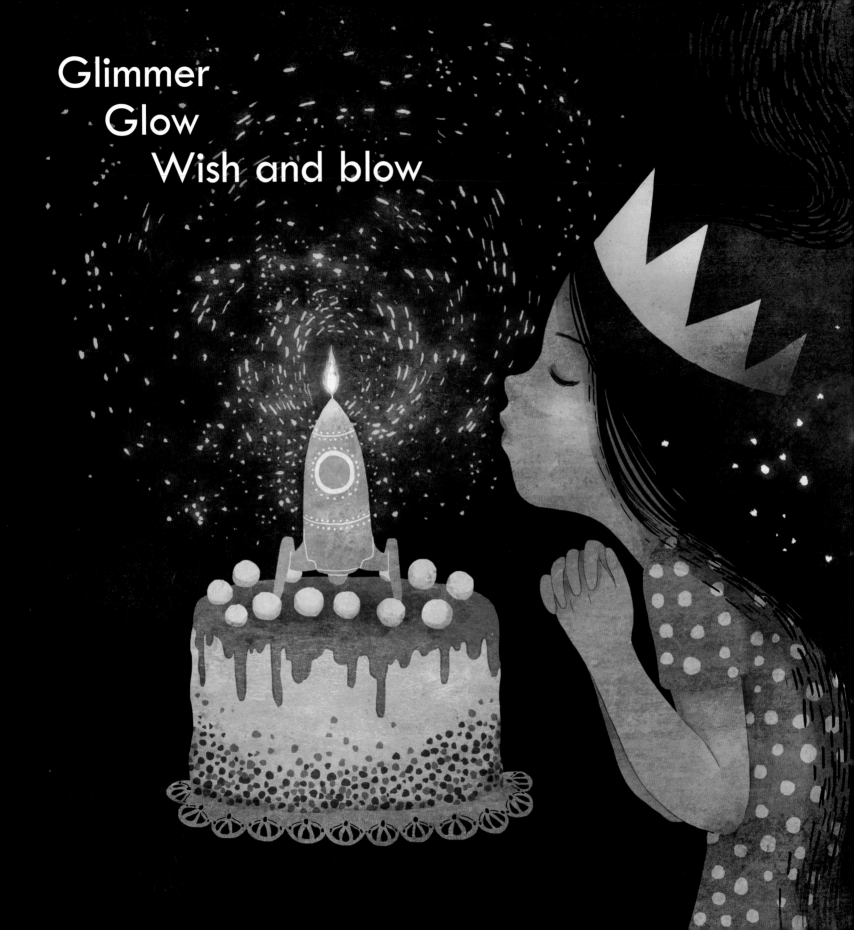

Glimmer
Glow
Wish and blow

Blast
Beam
Let us dream

Fade
Away
Cannot stay . . .

Swirl
Flow
Come and go

Flicker
Feel
Help us heal

Float
Guide
Far and wide

Blink
Play
Show the way

Shimmer
Glance
Blaze and dance

Soar
Wait . . .

Celebrate!

Spark
Fly
Fill the sky

Burst
Create
Illuminate

Bless
Shine
In a line

Dazzle
Thrill
Spread goodwill

Gleam
Bright . . .
Say good night.

THE SCIENCE OF LIGHT

What Is Light?

Light is a form of energy. We see the light of different energies as different colors. Red is lower-energy light, and blue is higher-energy light. White light is a combination of all the colors of the rainbow! When white light passes through a *prism*, a thick piece of glass, usually triangular in shape, the light is separated into its individual colors and we see a rainbow.

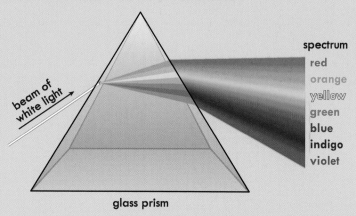

beam of white light

spectrum
red
orange
yellow
green
blue
indigo
violet

glass prism

Light moves very fast! It travels 186,000 miles (299,338 km) every second. Our Sun is 93 million miles (150 million km) away. This means that it takes eight minutes for light to travel from the Sun to Earth. Wow!

The biggest source of light on our world is the Sun. The Sun is a star, which is an enormous ball of very hot gases. As the star uses its fuel of hydrogen, it makes energy in the form of light and heat. This sunlight warms Earth, creates the weather, and is key to photosynthesis—which is when plants and some organisms use sunlight to grow.

Let's look at some other light:

FUN FACT
The scientific term for light is *electromagnetic radiation*. This is because light is made up of electric and magnetic energy. *Radiation* just means that the light energy travels outward from its source in a straight path.

Lightning

Lightning is a powerful movement of static electricity. It's a giant electrical spark, caused when thunderclouds separate positive and negative charges. Most lightning happens within the cloud, but sometimes you can see it happening between the cloud and the ground. These are called lightning strikes.

Rainbows

A rainbow is formed when sunlight shines on tiny droplets of water in the air. The water droplets act as miniature prisms, separating the sunlight into colors and reflecting the light back toward you. The colors are always the same, but the length and clarity of a rainbow depend on the size and number of the water droplets in the air.

The Northern Lights

The northern lights are natural displays of colored light—or auroras—that appear in the night sky, and they're magnificent! Auroras are caused by collisions between electrically charged particles from the Sun and Earth's air. The auroras that occur in the Northern

FUN FACT
Plants cannot "eat" green light. They reflect it away. This is why plants look green!

FUN FACT
When you are looking at a rainbow, the sun is always directly behind you!

Hemisphere are called the northern lights, or aurora borealis. (When they occur in the Southern Hemisphere, they're called aurora australis.) Auroras take many shapes and forms and may look like arcs, shimmering waves, or bands, and they change as the light moves across the sky.

Fireflies

Fireflies use special cells inside their bellies. Oxygen and other chemicals mix with a chemical called luciferin in the cells, which creates light through a chemical reaction known as bioluminescence. Fireflies talk to one another with their light signals. The pattern of blinking can mean several different things, such as defending a territory or trying to attract a mate.

Moonlight

The Moon is the brightest object seen in the night sky. While the Moon looks as if it is shining, it does not produce its own visible light—rather, it reflects sunlight! Sunlight lights up half of the Moon. When we can see the bright side of the Moon, it is called a full Moon. When we can see half of the bright side and half of the dark side, we call it a quarter Moon. The cycle of phases takes about a month because that is how long it takes for the Moon to orbit Earth.

LIGHT AND CELEBRATION

The **Fourth of July**, or Independence Day, is a holiday where Americans celebrate the United States' independence from Great Britain. To celebrate, people set off different colored fireworks. Sometimes communities hold parades or picnics, and there may be concerts featuring patriotic songs.

Yi Peng is one of Thailand's most spectacular celebrations. During the November festival, people launch thousands of fire-powered rice paper sky lanterns (called *khom loi*) into the air for good luck. The sky appears to be full of floating, burning stars.

Diwali, also called Dipawali, or the Festival of Lights, is a joyful Hindu holiday in October or November. It is the biggest holiday of the year in India and is celebrated by Hindus worldwide. This five-day holiday is a celebration—of light over darkness and good over evil. Families set clay oil lamps (called *deepa,* or *diya*) outside their homes to symbolize the inner light that protects them from spiritual darkness. People hang strings of lights outside their homes, and there are often fireworks displays and bonfires too!

Hanukkah, also called the Festival of Lights, is a Jewish holiday honoring the Maccabees's victory over King Antiochus, who forbade Jews to practice their religion. The victory allowed them to take back the Temple and practice their religion again. During Hanukkah, Jewish people light candles in a menorah with a helper candle called a shamash, every night at sundown for eight nights. The holiday celebrates the power of even a small light to overcome darkness.

Christmas is a Christian holiday that celebrates the birth of Jesus Christ. Around the world, friends and family members gather to exchange gifts, sing carols, and decorate the Christmas tree and home with lights. During the four Sundays leading up to Christmas, called Advent, and on Christmas Eve, many people go to church. Children wait for Santa Claus to come from the North Pole in a sleigh to deliver gifts.

For Kwame, Mary, and Anne Marie —S.F.

To my cats, for always being my
biggest fans and sticking by my
side for spiritual support during all
those late-night deadlines —K.L.

Special thanks to Dr. Crystal Pierce (Astrophysics),
for reviewing the text and illustrations.

Additional thanks to cultural consultants Ravi Chohan,
Ritika Sharma, Alex Sukhtipyaroge, Joni Sussman.

Millbrook Press™
An imprint of Lerner Publishing Group, Inc.
241 First Avenue North
Minneapolis, MN 55401 USA

For reading levels and more information, look up this title at www.lernerbooks.com.

Prism diagram by Laura Westlund/Independent Picture Service.

Designed by Lindsey Owens.
Main body text set in Tw Cen MT Std Medium. Typeface provided by Monotype Typography.
The illustrations in this book were created with mixed media and Photoshop.

Library of Congress Cataloging-in-Publication Data

Names: Fliess, Sue, illustrator. | Le, Khoa, 1982– illustrator.
Title: Flash and gleam : light in our world / Sue Fliess ; illustrated by Khoa Le.
Description: Minneapolis : Millbrook Press, [2020] | Audience: Ages 5–8. | Audience: K to grade 3.
Identifiers: LCCN 2019012022 (print) | LCCN 2019013566 (ebook) | ISBN 9781541581173 (eb pdf) |
    ISBN 9781541557703 (lb : alk. paper)
Subjects: LCSH: Light—Miscellanea—Juvenile literature.
Classification: LCC QC360 (ebook) | LCC QC360 .F55 2020 (print) | DDC 535—dc23

LC record available at https://lccn.loc.gov/2019012022

Manufactured in the United States of America
1-46165-45959-8/2/2019